The

Gifted

Teen Edition

Julia A. Royston

ROYSTON
Publishing

BK Royston Publishing
P. O. Box 4321
Jeffersonville, IN 47131
502-802-5385
http://bkroystonpublishing.com
bkroystonpublishing@gmail.com

Published by: BK Royston Publishing LLC

ISBN-13: 9781688259591

Printed in the United States of America

To Every Gifted Child in the World. May You Always Use Your Gift and Be Great.

Acknowledgement

I thank my Lord and Savior Jesus Christ for giving me another opportunity to introduce more people to you. I thank you that you have entrusted this gift to me.

To my husband, Brian K. Royston, the love of my life for loving and cheering me on so much that I can be and do all that God has placed in me. I love you...

To my Mom, who is a great support and to my Dad who is in heaven but, I know is proud of me and always encouraged me to go for it. Thanks to all of my family for their love and support.

A special thank you to Rev. and Mrs. Claude R. Royston for their love and support.

I dedicate this book to every

gifted person in the world. No matter what that gift is it is key to the movement, motivation and multiplication of the Kingdom. Stir up your gift and use it for God's Glory. Remember, "You are Gifted." God Bless You in all that you for the King and His Kingdom.

Love, Julia A. Royston

Table of Contents

Introduction

When I was eight years old, I literally imagined how my life would be. I didn't understand it all at eight, but I had a vivid imagination. I would spend hours in my family's basement, listening to music and imagining that one day that I would be a singer, travel, teach, and get paid to do it. It was incredible. I had so much fun. I didn't spend hours by myself because my life was horrible. Far from it. I had two loving parents, two annoying sisters, and a wonderful childhood. We worked hard, traveled everywhere, and lived a wonderful life, for real. So, don't get it twisted that my life was so bad that I needed an escape. Nope, I just needed space to dream. Why? Because I was going to have to know myself and what I wanted for my life and not depend on my parents to tell me what that life should be and look like. Low and behold (yes that's an old people's term), I am living the life that I only dreamed about right now. At the writing of this book, I am fifty-six years old and living what I only dreamed about. Now, my current life added more things to it. First, I have written fifty-five books. Second, I write, record, and perform my own music. Third, I own two publishing companies as well as a music publishing company for my music. My eight-year old dream has expanded in a HUGE way, but it is my way. Finally, I am retired from a full-time job and just run my businesses full-time. I am living my dream. This dream started when I was eight. There were some twists, turns, changes, and revisits to my dream, but it happened. I want it to happen for you too. You are creative, gifted, and talented, and can achieve anything you set your mind to do. I believe that and I hope this book will help you live out that dream.

Let's go!

Julia Royston

There's a gift inside

No matter what age you are reading this book, I believe that there is something special inside of you that is unique to only you. I call it a gift. I believe that each and every one of us is born with a gift, talent, or natural ability to do something. Others may do the same thing that you do, but it is not the same as when you do it. Have you ever seen a person who sings and they can sing well? But there is something about when someone else sings the same song, in the same key, with the right words, and same phrasing that makes the song sound different. That is a gift. There are some people who can be taught to sing and others who are gifted to sing. No training, no voice lessons, no coaching, or extra help, but they can open their mouths and just sing and bring tears to your eyes or chills down your spine. That's a gift. Singing is my love and passion and my first gift. That's the reason why I refer to singing so much. Your gift doesn't have to be anything related to music at all.

My first, natural-born gift was to sing. I realized that at the age of eight. It was like breathing. I enjoyed music at an even earlier age of three, but my voice came in the junior choir at my church. When I finished singing, the people in the church were on their feet. My parents and everyone there recognized it. I did too. It kind of scared me, but I remembered all of the time I practiced in the basement and knew that I was ready for that song at least.

I know that my gift is still to sing, but more important than the gift is the ability to learn, be taught, and take what I learned and apply it to my natural-born gifts and abilities. You see, no matter what your gift is, it has to be molded, made, and trained to be the best that it can be prior to being presented to the world. Gifts still have to be cultivated, worked on, or developed. It's like getting a gift at Christmas, but it requires setup, assembly, or having the batteries added. You have everything to make it go, but there are some missing parts, pieces, or things that you have to do to make the gift work best.

But first, you have to know what your gift is. My gift arrived and came easily because it was my love, passion, and joy. I loved music and fortunately, early on, music loved me back.   Music was that thing that nobody had to make me do. I didn't need prompting, encouragement to study or to be told constantly to practice. I wanted to do it. Loved to sing. Loved to listen to new music that came out. I knew you could get paid to sing, but I would sing even if they didn't pay me. That's when you know it is real love. When you want to do something, legally, that even if they didn't pay you, you would do. That's one key. Passion.

Secondly, a gift is something that you do well. You didn't earn the gift, but you still have to work hard to maintain it. The gift you have comes out easily. It takes little effort and people enjoy it coming from you. Your gift may not be perfect compared to others with the same gift that have been doing it for many years and are more experienced, but we all can see it when you utilize your gift. Go back to your Christmas presents I talked about earlier. What if you threw your brand-new Christmas Day gift in the fireplace? It wouldn't work too well, would it? You couldn't get the enjoyment out of your gift if you threw it in a place of destruction, could you? So, a gift is not only a passion and something you love, but something that you don't take for granted, will cherish, and will take care of. I will discuss how important this is later, but for now, know that it is something that you do well and will argue or fight anyone about if challenged.

Finally, your gift is something that you can profit from. I believe that a gift is that thing that you can always do well, but someone will pay you to do that gift. I believe that everyone has a divine, money-generating ability down in them so that you will never be broke a day in your life. That's just the way I believe. I've seen it happen too many times in too many people.

So, what do you believe is your gift? What do you do well that you love and that people also enjoy? If you don't know what your gift is, ask somebody, "What do you believe that I am gifted to do?"

What is Your Gift?

Reflection

_____

_____

_____

_____

_____

_____

_____

_____

_____

_____

_____

_____

_____

_____

School: Gift Activator

I loved school. I don't know what it was, but I really liked school. I didn't have an easy time in school, but I loved to learn. Remember I said that I believe my first natural gift was to learn? School was where I came into my own. Sure, you might say that I was going to like school no matter what because my father was a teacher. But that is not so since just because your parents do something or have a natural ability to do something or are gifted in an area doesn't automatically mean that you will do the same thing. We'll talk about that later, but right now, it's school. Now some of you are rolling your eyes and sucking your teeth or almost wanting to close this book because you hate school. But don't close it yet. Just in case you don't know what your gift is and how to even use it, school is the free gift activator.

Two ways. First, in school, you will find out if some subject or activity stimulates you, you like it and do very well in that subject or activity. Secondly, school will help you determine if no subject areas interest you, and if the thing, activity, program, or project that you really like is something else. What I mean is, school will help you find out what you like or are gifted to do, or do not like or want to do. In other words, it will either show you what you can do well or will love to do or it will show you what you really don't want to do and you will be drawn to what you really want to do, whether this thing is in school or out of school. Now, let me pause right here to say, make sure your gift is for good and not bad. You are old enough to know what that means. If not, let me explain it to you. If your gift seems to cause you to be in an alternative school, in the principal's office, or thrown out of the classroom or other public places, this is NOT the type of gift that I am talking about. I am talking about a gift that you would be proud to do in front of your grandmother, nana, or big mama. You got it? I thought so, let's move on. Now I know that you've heard comedians talk about being thrown out of classrooms for talking too much or making kids laugh in class. That too is a gift, but it must be controlled. Just because you are great at something doesn't mean you need to show off that gift everywhere you go and at all times. I love to sing, but there are times to sing and then there are times to be quiet and listen. There are opportunities for me to use my gift, which is great, but there are other times when it's not my turn, but someone else's turn to use their gift. Got it? I knew you would.

In conclusion, use school as a test market for your gift in a good and positive way. Not destructive or combative, but so that in the end, it will be great that you were a part of that school. It will also be a springboard into other opportunities. Activate your gift.

What is Your Favorite Subject in School?

_____

_____

_____

_____

_____

_____

_____

_____

_____

_____

_____

_____

_____

_____

_____

_____

_____

_____

_____

The Family Business vs. Your Gift

This is a tough chapter for me because I was always the kid who did what my parents said. I rarely got disciplined because I didn't like spankings or time-out you may be too young people to have experienced either. You may find that the family business is right in line with your gift or your abilities. You could actually help the family business. That is something for you to determine. I also know that some of your parents want you to take over their business one day and are almost forcing you to want what they want instead of what you want. Let me tell you my story.

My father was a teacher, but in the evenings, as well as every day, he had a janitor service. Growing up, my mom took care of the business during the day while my sisters and I were in school and my dad taught school. In the evenings, on the weekends, or any other time, we helped with the business. It allowed us to have a wonderful life with all types of extras that we enjoyed. As we got older and went to college, we had our own interests. Before graduating high school, we worked in the business, of course. I took typing in high school. So, I typed all of the contracts, monthly invoices, and any other correspondence. That was my job. I had no interest in the janitor company other than helping my parents. Cleaning wasn't my natural gift. It was learned and demanded of me because I lived in my parents' house.

Although my parents were fully supportive of our pursuits, if I knew then what I know now, I would have taken over my parents' business instead of pursuing the things I wanted and hired someone to do the work and I would have just managed it. I didn't see that far in advance and how my life was going to turn out. I am a natural manager. Although I am gifted in singing, I am also gifted in business, and I am organized.

I want you to do things differently than me or anyone else. I want you to pursue your dreams, be GREAT at them, and be profitable at THEM. Use your gifts in the family business, if they apply. Support and love your parents. Let your parents guide, advise, and support you. They really do love you even if they don't understand you. Learn all that your parents are trying to teach you.

Knowing multiple things never hurt anybody, but also know what your gift and passion is in your life because as you get older and are able to make your own decisions, it will be your choice, your right, and your need to Fight for Your Life.

Family Business Vs. Your Gift - Which will you choose?

Fight for Your Life

I said these exact words to a young person. They had graduated from college and their life wasn't matching up with their parents' expectations. Nothing bad really. The person was working and trying to find better work, not doing anything illegal, immoral, or wrong, but they weren't living up to their parents' expectations. The young person was trying to find themselves and navigate the world, but they weren't moving fast enough to get the dream job, house, and car that their parents had imagined for them. The person was talented, gifted, operating in their gift, and doing all they knew, but the economy and job opportunities weren't cooperating. This is part two to the previous chapter.

What is the solution? My grandfather had a saying, "I can show you better than I can tell you." Show them. Prove it. It is hard to complain about, compete with or stop success. When you are doing what you love, are successful at it, and others recognize it, your parents will probably come on board. But you first have to fight for it. You've got to do it. You've got to be consistent at it, especially if it is NOT the family business.

I know a young woman who is an excellent musician. She has a degree in music. She teaches music, but that is definitely NOT the path her parents wanted. Why? Music is a very risky profession. It is competitive. It is low paying or no paying when you start out unless you catch a break, are fortunate, and are in the right place at the right time. This person worked hard, honed her craft, and travels the world with her music. Was it fun trying to convince her parents? No. Is it painful doing something you love without the support of the people you love the most? Of course. In the end, being true to yourself or walking in your truth and fighting for YOUR life is what's important. Now I caution you to do this fully when you are able to survive on your own, just in case this truth might get you thrown out of the house. BUT, in the end, you have to live with yourself, your choices, and your decisions.

On the other hand, you may find that your parents' business, suggestions, and opportunities work for you. That is okay too. But you make that decision and then you can live better with the decision you make. Whatever decision you make, fight for it. Work for it. Be the best at that thing that you love and are gifted to do. When you do what you do and only how you can do it, nobody can deny you. Fight for your gift and your life.

What Are You Fighting For? Write it on the Gloves.

Remain Open

One final thought on choosing your path for your life and using your gifts: always remain open. Don't shut yourself off to new ideas, methods, strategies, or ways of doing anything. You have to remember that older people have been down the road a few times or lived life longer and may know a few more things that you don't. Stop. Listen. Learn.

The elders in my day used to say, "Eat the meat and spit out the bones." In today's terms, take what they say and use what applies to you and if it doesn't apply to you, store it because you may need it sometime later in life. Timing is everything. Some things people say you don't understand at first, but remember it, think about it, and store it because you "just never know."

When utilizing your gift, you have to be okay with helpful criticism, instruction, opportunities, and coaching. Some people are your formal coaches and other people are informal coaches. That means you will have coaches that you hire or want to have in your life and there will be other coaches who assign themselves to you because they want to see you do well and be the best. Don't shut any of it out. Using the meat and bones reference, get what you need and store or discard what doesn't work for you. You can learn something from everyone. From a small child to an adult, there is something a person can offer to make you better.

It is left up to you to accept it or reject the advice they offer. Remaining open keeps you from getting stale, stagnant, or stuck in one place and never moving forward. I realize for this generation, you are always on the move, but if you are like me, you like the "comfort zone." Even though I'm always on the move, I like stability and don't enjoy much change. But change is a part of life. You can't grow unless you change. You can't get better unless you change. You can't know more unless you decide to learn, go to school and class, and make the changes necessary to succeed. There is a classic and very old song that starts, "Everything must change, nothing stays the same." It is a true song. Yes, I know it's true because I'm older, but you can learn these lessons as a younger person and save yourself a lot of heartache. Remain Open.

What are You Passionate About?

Reflection

_____

_____

_____

_____

_____

_____

_____

_____

_____

_____

_____

_____

_____

_____

_____

_____

Stay in School – Learning Takes a Lifetime.

Learning is a Lifelong Journey, not to be done or finished in twelve years of formal education or an additional four to eight years of postsecondary education. You are never done with school, learning, or educating or training yourself. Always be someone who is teachable and learning something new from someone. In my day, I wanted to be better at singing without getting hoarse or having my voice going out after singing two songs. I didn't take voice lessons to learn how to sing. I could sing already, but I needed to know how to use the gift, instrument, and ability that I already had and make it better. I took voice lessons for three years from a professional opera singer. It was wonderful. I learned so much from her, but there came a time when she asked me to stop singing in my church choir and only sing classical music. I refused and we parted ways. I paid her the fee and didn't reschedule my next session. I didn't bash her or call her names or write her a dirty note. Why? I learned a lot, but our season was over. I would need to find another teacher or someone who could help me with my particular singing style and current level of singing.

I still utilize the things she taught me to this day. With the advances in technology, you might be able to get the help you need via pre-recorded videos on YouTube, Facebook Groups, or by watching others. I learned a lot from sitting still and watching others hone and work their gift.

Know this, you do have to perfect, work, study, research, and develop your gift. Just like a seed, you have to water it, make sure that there are no weeds or bugs to attack it to kill it, and put it in the environment so that it will get the light, sunshine, opportunity, and encouragement that it needs to grow. It's a fact.

Finally, you have to have your gift around other gifted, like-minded, non-jealous, or non-gift-killing people and most definitely, people who have the same work ethic as you do to stimulate you and help you grow your gift. It's just a fact.

Reflection

_____

_____

_____

_____

_____

_____

_____

_____

_____

_____

_____

_____

_____

_____

Who do You Hang Out With?

I am not trying to get in your business. Who you hang around with is your business and yours alone, but let me give you some things to think about. Who you hang around will affect, impact, and influence whether you succeed in life. I know your parents tell you that all of the time and you roll your eyes, quietly ignore them, and go back to your phone or other mobile device, but it is true. The old saying, "Birds of a feather flock together" is true. If you hang around with people who do bad things enough, you will either do those same bad things or if caught, be accused of doing those bad things. It can happen. You don't have to do the bad thing to be accused of it if someone in your group has done something wrong.

So, who are your friends? What do they like to do? Where do they spend their time and energy? Do they have college on their vision board? What are their grades? What are their gifts? When you are born, you don't pick your family, but you do pick your friends. Now you can pick some new family members later, but when you are born, you have the family that you have. Check out your circle of friends. Even as an adult, I have to check and re-check my circle of friends. There are close friends, acquaintances, and people I know in the world. I know that sounds terrible, but when you have goals, dreams, and visions of where you want to be in life, you have to put the people in your life into categories. These categories can change sometimes based on the seasons, situations, and settings in your life. I have one best friend who says that even if I try to dump her, she is not going anywhere. I agree and she will be in the best friend category for life. But she still doesn't go with me everywhere because she has a life of her own. She has dreams, goals, and visions of her own. I support and love her and she supports and loves me. I'm not saying that you have to dump all of your friends or take all of your friends with you on every step of your journey, but you have to be careful who is on your team. Jealousy is a horrible thing and can make people do and say things that they wouldn't normally say or do.

I have a small circle of close friends and even some family members that I truly trust. It is hard, but I knew as a child that I was gifted.

My parents told me so and I had to learn about trusting people the hard way. My job now is to help others not make the same mistakes I did or see the potential mistakes before they happen to them.

Check your circle. Who are you hanging out with?

Who is in Your Circle?

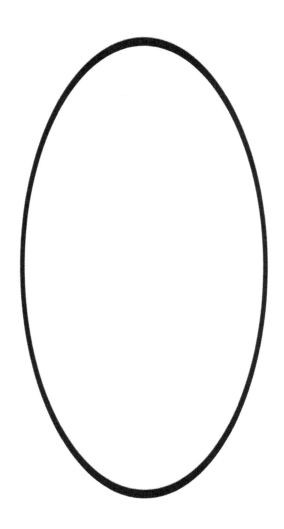

Did you know you can make money at_____?

When thinking about your gifts, talents, and abilities, take the statement out of your vocabulary, "I don't know any job where I can do this."

Being gifted is not necessarily about getting a job, but about doing your best at what you do, people wanting and needing what you do, you charging a fee, and getting paid for what you do. I don't know of a job that is specifically called "writing coach," but I do it every day. I work from home or anywhere in the world. I don't punch a clock. I help people in person, on live or pre-recorded videos to produce the books that they desire. I no longer have to leave my house to go to another building to get paid to do something that I am good at. I can do it anywhere in the world with an internet connection, Wi-Fi, my phone, my laptop, and my webcam. It's that easy. I can run an entire company through my phone and laptop. You can too.

But we have to go back to the first question I asked in the book: what is your gift or what do you love to do?

_____

_____

_____

_____

_____

_____

_____

_____

_____

_____

_____

_____

_____

_____

_____

_____

Reflection

_____

_____

_____

_____

_____

_____

_____

_____

_____

_____

_____

_____

_____

_____

You are Limited Only by You

In the previous chapter, we talked about who is in your circle of friends or who you hang out with. That is important and I don't want you to overlook that chapter. You should take a hard look at the friends you keep. I know that bullying is a serious subject and a lot of attention is placed on bullying. If you need help, be sure to tell, tell, and tell again. Tell your parents, tell the teacher, tell a police officer, tell the principal, tell and tell again. It is not cool to not feel safe by having someone else harassing you.

Your job at this age is to enjoy life, learn all you can, be who were meant to be and grow. There is help out there for you. Access the help and exercise your rights. Finally, I don't care if it is an adult, child, young adult, teacher, male, or female. If they are NOT treating you as they should, TELL.

With all of that being said, you can't let anything stop you. No matter if what happened is good, bad, or ugly, you have to keep going, dreaming, and using your gift. I realize that when you are underage, there are some things you can't do on your own. But after you are an adult, there is nothing and no one that can stop you but you. You are not limited by anyone else, no matter who they are and how they are connected to you. Remember that the only person that can really stop you is you. Now, people may slow you, make your life hard, or put blocks in your way, but in the end, get up, re-group, get the help that you need, and keep going toward your goal.

There are some people in this world that make it their life's ambition to stop you. They speak all types of negative things. They point out the one hundred things about your idea that won't work, but never seem to point out the ten things that WILL work. They have no other motive than trying to stop you. You may call them a hater, but I feel like these people are worse than that because they have their own life, but they are spending the time that they should be working on themselves, worrying about you. Yuck! Get your own life! Okay I said it. But what now? It hurt me. I didn't like what they said. It still hurts even after they have stopped talking. You are right and have every reason to feel the way you do. What is the best way to get even? Complete the project. Launch the idea. Be successful. Go for it!

Reflection

_____

_____

_____

_____

_____

_____

_____

_____

_____

_____

_____

_____

_____

_____

What's Next? – Plan Your Work & Work Your Plan

If you are in school or still school-aged, the number one goal is to do well in your classes. Focus, study, and get the help that you need to complete school. No matter if it is middle school, high school, or college, focus on that. That's first. Why? It is the foundation for life. Whether you hate, like, or love school, it is your right as a citizen to get an education. Remember what I said earlier: eat the meat or get what you can, spit out the bones, and don't worry about the rest.

Do your best. Turn in the assignments. Pass the test. It will teach you determination, endurance, and discipline. You are gifted. You need to be able to read well so you can read those multi-million-dollar contracts that are coming your way. You need to be able to write well and make the demands necessary for you, your gift, and your future companies. You need to be able to do math so that you can count the money you will make in your lifetime. I speak it into existence. Remember I didn't say anything about a job, but if you have to get a job, be able to read the application, complete it, and do the job that they are paying you to do. I have had many jobs in my lifetime. I don't down anyone for having a job. A job is what financed my dream, but when the job doesn't pay enough or closes, I want you to be able to continue to make money until the next job or until you open up your own business and eventually, the empire.

Next, when school is not in session, keep yourself on the lookout for other opportunities. There are camps, free classes, and online YouTube videos that can help you to learn more about what you are gifted to do. In my life, I have been the queen of watching what others do and then create it for myself. I didn't have the benefit of YouTube or social media to learn new ideas or tasks. I had to literally watch people in my church, in my community, on television, or pay for coaching and classes. There is so much free information, tutoring, and mentoring out here, it is amazing. Don't sleep on the free public library that is at your disposal. Remember to check your circle of so-called friends. If they tease you, downplay you, or make you feel badly in any way for pursuing your dreams, dump them. I will repeat it, "DUMP THEM." They are NOT your friends. They are dream killers! Sure, speak, be cordial, but don't waste time trying to make people understand you, agree with you, support you, or cheer for you and your gift. Show them! My grandfather said it best, "I can show you better than I can tell you." Again, Show THEM!

Finally, I have never had a time in my life that there wasn't someone that came along to help me. Sometimes they have come in the most unlikely place and been an unexpected person. Remember your help may not know you, look like you, or you may not know them, but divinely they are sent to help you. You will recognize them immediately. They will help you freely, with no questions, no strings attached, or no favors needed in return, just the help, information, or answer to the question you need to get you to the next level, space, or place.

If nothing else, the help will point you in the direction that you need to go. Even if they don't know the answer to the question, they'll say, "Go there and ask them and see if they can help."

Don't overlook counselors, therapists, librarians, teachers, administrators, or other public servants who are in a position to help. If one doesn't help, keep going to the next person.

If you are under the age of eighteen, I need for your parent or guardian to reach out to me and I can help point you both in the right direction. Check me out on YouTube or social media. I have online and LIVE events periodically that help authors, business owners, and non-profit organizations with writing, publishing, and promoting and producing other products and services. Don't sleep on your gift. Don't worry about how you start, just start.   Start in your bedroom.   Start in your parents' basement. Start in your school, but be sure and put your gift to work. Work toward your dream one step at a time and one day at a time.

Where do we start? Right here.

When do we start? Right now.

Made in the USA
Monee, IL
19 August 2021